SONGBIRD

Immy Burke

As you sing

9 secular concert works for upper voices

COMPILED BY
Neil Ferris and
Joanna Tomlinson

OXFORD

OXFORD
UNIVERSITY PRESS

Great Clarendon Street, Oxford OX2 6DP,
United Kingdom

Oxford University Press is a department of the University of Oxford.
It furthers the University's objective of excellence in research, scholarship,
and education by publishing worldwide. Oxford is a registered trade mark of
Oxford University Press in the UK and in certain other countries

First published 2018

Impression: 1

ISBN 978-0-19-352421-7

Music and text origination by
Katie Johnston
Printed in Great Britain on acid-free paper by
Halstan & Co. Ltd, Amersham, Bucks.

Contents

Notes on the pieces

As you sing   *Sarah Quartel*

This is the piece that inspired the title of the collection. The text is full of the joy of singing, and this is a fast, fun, and energetic song that would work well as the first or last piece in a concert. Be sure to check that the repeated 'la's don't get overworked: the tongue movements for the 'l' should be fast and free. Although the tempo is fast, the lines are long and flowing; stay well-connected and smooth through the syncopations in the melody.

The silver swan   *Oliver Tarney*

This is an exquisitely beautiful and haunting setting of *The silver swan* that would fit any programme around the themes of nature, life, love, and loss. The melody should be sung with a flowing line: keep the breath moving. Take care that the low Es in the octave leaps are not sung with too much heavy chest-voice, otherwise the top E will sound strained.

'Hope' is the thing with feathers   *Michael Higgins*

This is a beautiful and imaginative setting of Emily Dickinson's poem that also gives the accompanist a wonderful part to play. While it is not complicated, it nevertheless requires particular attention to the text and long legato lines, making sure that the four-bar phrases are sung in one breath; this is possible if the tempo indication is observed. Take care of the rhythm coming off the tie in the opening phrase; it has to be smooth but also in time.

Fly away, fly away over the sea   *Russell Hepplewhite*

The opening section of this song perfectly captures the elements of nostalgia and loss. This is contrasted well with the urgency of a fast, syncopated middle section. In the opening section, take care of the long 'eh' vowel each time on 'away'. Sing on a clean 'eh', and tuck the diphthong in at the end. In the fast section, be careful to observe the different dynamic levels so that the sense of anticipation and urgency is maintained.

Charm   *Kerry Andrew*

This is a thrilling and unusual piece, with some very funky riffs. Don't be afraid to be free and imaginative with the speaking at the beginning and how you might perform the ingredients being tossed into the cauldron! You can also be flexible about moving your singers from one vocal (or whistling) part to another to get a good balance between the lines. Sing with freedom and energy, and explore the colours in the voice to bring out some of the textures.

Sweet and low   *Andy Brooke*

Sweet and low is an appealing and gentle lullaby with a wonderfully catchy melody. It is beautifully crafted and has an enjoyable simplicity about it, remaining in two parts throughout. There is an opportunity to focus on bringing the text to the fore, with plenty of alliteration: 'breathe, blow' and 'wind, western'. Use the comma each time text is repeated, for example 'low, low', to help the clarity of the words.

Now is the time   *Cecilia McDowall*

This is a moving anthem-like setting of words by Marie Curie—profound and thought-provoking. There is a strength and resolve about the melody at the words 'Now is the time', and the piece gives an opportunity to explore unifying themes of life and its struggles, but also spirit and determination. Aim for a warm, rich sound, and, where possible, quick top-up breaths should be taken to ensure that the quality of sound is consistent throughout the longer phrases.

This we know   *Sarah Quartel*

The global message of this piece is movingly conveyed with pop-like harmonies and simple and accessible vocal lines. The large range of dynamics should be carefully observed, and the crescendos and diminuendos carefully paced. The word 'know' is repeated several times: be careful not to move to the 'ooh' part of the diphthong until the end of the note. Make sure the middle section is taken quickly enough, and explore a different vocal colour: a darker and richer sonority is needed here.

Give me the river   *Toby Young*

This is a thrilling, high-energy piece that includes body-percussion and sound effects to convey the atmosphere of the fast-moving river—a superb finale or encore in a concert. Some of the rhythms in the chorus look challenging on the page, but they repeat and may be best learned by ear. The melody needs to be sung with attention to the line, despite the fact that it looks very rhythmical. This will help bring out the text and give a sense of being carried along on the powerful river current.

Neil Ferris and Joanna Tomlinson

Commissioned by Village Voices, Seer Green, Buckinghamshire; Jane Smith, conductor

As you sing

Words and music by
SARAH QUARTEL
(b. 1982)

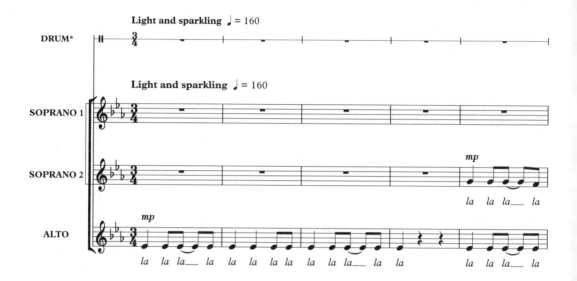

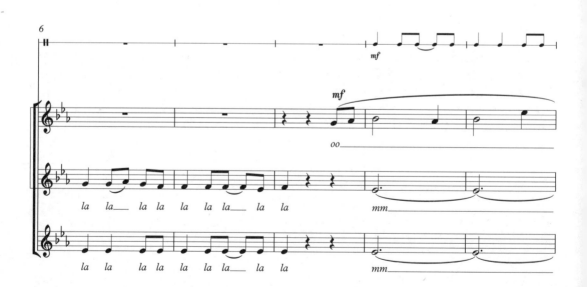

Duration: 3 mins

* Any hand drum with a warm sound.

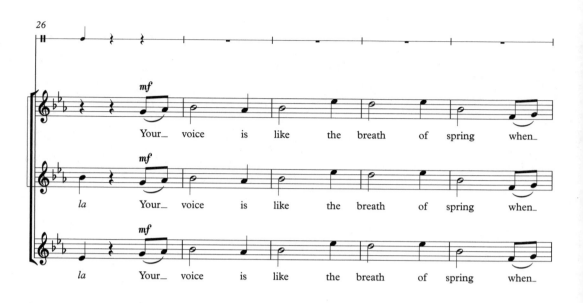

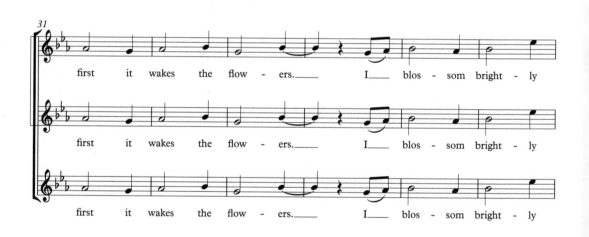

121

la_____ la_____

la_____ la

cher - ry___ tree.   I   shine   when   you   are   near._____

126

mp

mf

la   Your_ voice   is   like   an   an - cient   oak   that_ stands   in

mp

la   oo_____

mp

___   oo_____

132

gen - tle   strength._____   My_ roots   run   deep - er   as   you   sing.

ah_____

ah_____

The silver swan

English text by Anon. (adap.)

OLIVER TARNEY
(b. 1984)

Duration: 4 mins

last, O— thus— sang she,— and sang— no more:

Fare - well, all joys, fare - well, all joys; O death, come close my—

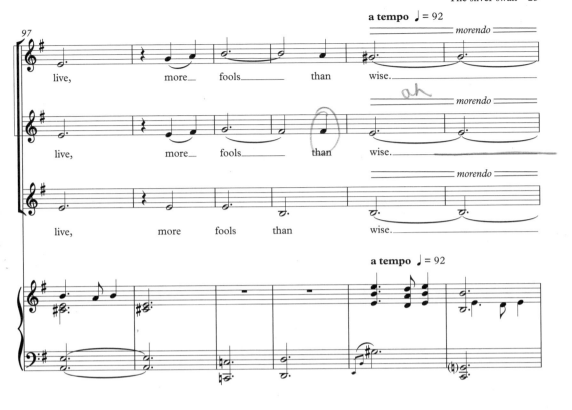

'Hope' is the thing with feathers

Emily Dickinson (1830–86)

MICHAEL HIGGINS
(b. 1981)

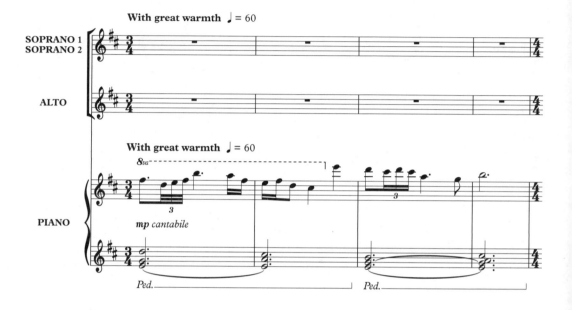

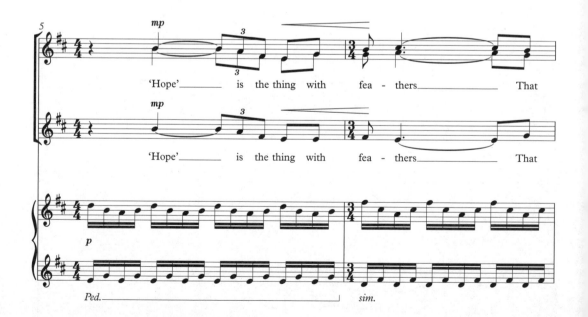

Duration: 3 mins

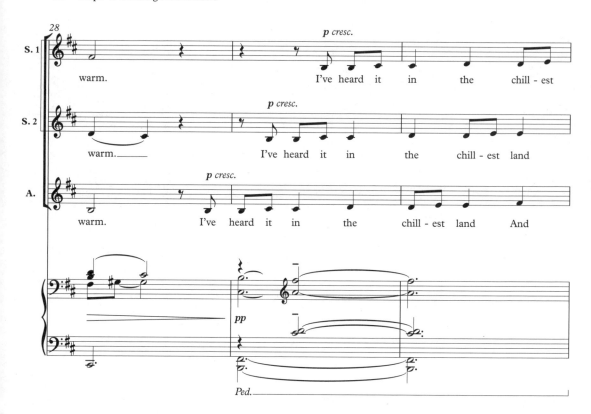

Fly away, fly away over the sea

Christina Rossetti (1830–94)

RUSSELL HEPPLEWHITE
(b. 1982)

Duration: 3 mins

Come a - gain,_ come back to me,_

_ come a - gain,_ come back to me,_

Come a - gain,_ come back to me,_

Come a - gain,_ come back to me,_

come   a - gain,_   come   back   to

Come   a - gain,_ come back   to   me,_____   come   back   to

Come   a - gain,_ come back   to   me,_____   come   back   to

me,_____

me,_____

me,_____

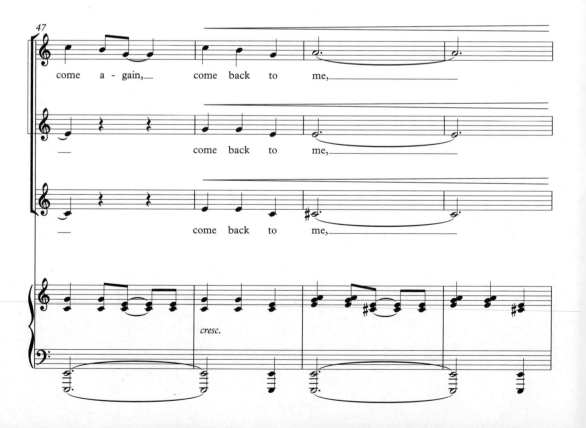

Bring - ing the sum - mer_____
Bring - ing the

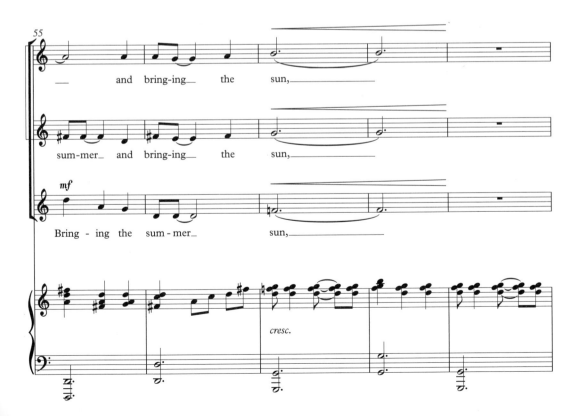

_____ and bring-ing____ the sun,_____
sum-mer____ and bring-ing____ the sun,_____
Bring - ing the sum - mer____ sun,_____

cresc.

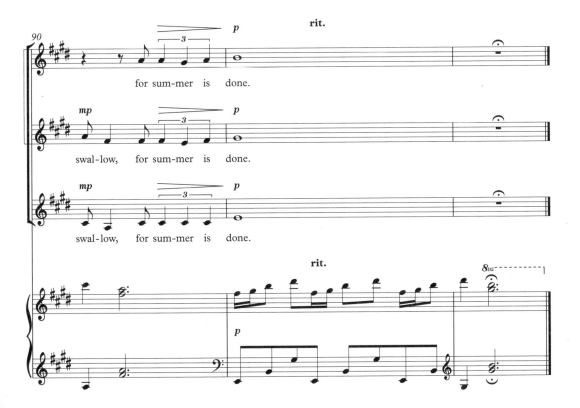

Anglo-Saxon metrical charms were sets of instructions that were meant to cure sickness or resolve troubles. They tended to include ingredients for potions, and were intended to be spoken aloud, with certain phrases to be repeated several times. Twelve such charms survive in Old English, including this one for water-elf disease, which involves watery eyes and pale, ill-looking nails.

Here, the composer has adapted the Old English into her own modern text, with two exceptions:

1) **'sing** þis **gealdor ofer** þriwa' (sing this charm three times) is retained, shown as it is to be pronounced: 'sing this gal-dor of-er thrir-wah'

2) the ingredients for the 'herb box whispers' sections at the beginning and end. At the conductor's discretion, each singer should choose 1–3 herbs from the list below and whisper them clearly, in their own time, with pauses in between. This may also be accompanied by optional movements, such as dropping a herb into a bowl each time a word is spoken.

eoforþrote (thistle) = a-yo-for-thro-the
cassuc (cassock) = cass-uk
fone nioþoweard (the lower part of an iris) = fon-eh nyo-thoh-wahrd
eowberge (yew berry) = a-yo-ber-geh
elehtre (lupine) = ay-lay(ch)[1]-treh
eolone (elecampane) = a-yo-lö[2]-neh
merscmealwan crop (marshmallow tops) = mehr-sh-mahl-wun-crop
fenminte (fen mint) = fayn-mint-eh
dile (dill) = dill-eh
lilie (lily) = li-ly
attorlaþe (betony) = ut-tor-luh-theh
polleie (pennyroyal) = poll-eh-y
marubie (horehound) = muh-roo-bee
docce (dock) = dock-eh
ellen (elder) = el-layn
felterre (centaury) = fel-ter-reh
wermod (wormwood) = wer-mod
streawbergean leaf (strawberry leaf) = strah-ber-gahn lahf
consolde (comfrey) = con-sol-deh

[1] (ch) = hard German 'ch' (as in loch)
[2] ö = German 'ö' (similar to the 'er' sound in English)

Charm

Anon., adap. Kerry Andrew

KERRY ANDREW
(b. 1978)

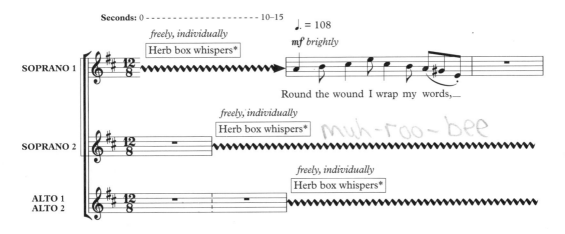

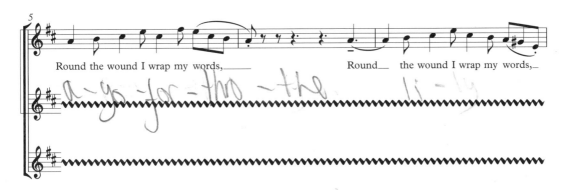

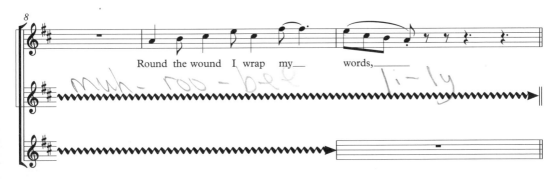

Duration: 2.5 mins

* = See notes.

for Bob Chilcott, Mavis Fletcher, and the ABCD North West Children's Honour Choir

Sweet and low

Alfred, Lord Tennyson
(1809–92)

ANDY BROOKE
(b. 1970)

Duration: 3 mins

Sleep__ and rest,   sleep__ and rest,

Sleep,   sleep__ and rest,   and rest,__

Fa - ther will come to thee soon;   Rest,__ rest,   on

Fa - ther will come to thee soon;   Rest,   rest,__ on

Now is the time

Marie Curie (1867–1934)

CECILIA McDOWALL
(b. 1951)

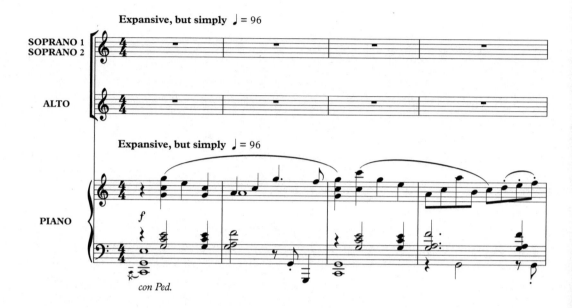

Duration: 3.5 mins

* The voice parts may be doubled by the piano, if desired.

Also available separately in an arrangement for SATB and piano (ISBN 978–0–19–351260–3).

Commissioned for the 2016 International Choral Kathaumixw; Paul Cummings, Artistic Director

This we know

Ted Perry
(Inspired by a speech given by Chief Seattle
in the 19th century)

SARAH QUARTEL
(b. 1982)

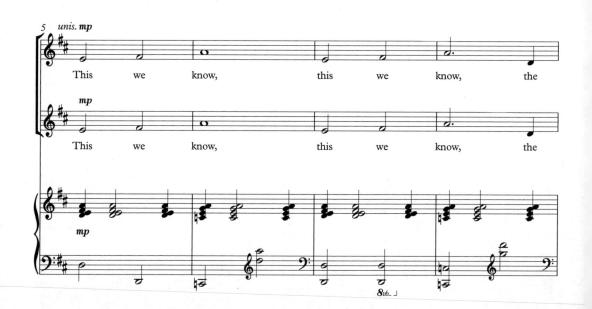

Duration: 3 mins

know, the earth does not be - long to us, the earth does not be -

know, the earth does not be - long to us, the earth does not be -

-long to us. This

-long to us. This

we know.

we know.

for David Ogden and the Bristol Youth Choir

Give me the river

Jennifer Thorp (b. 1988)

TOBY YOUNG
(b. 1990)

Duration: 2.5 mins

* *sh* = to simulate the noise of a river

† = clap

‡ = stamp

* Continue pattern of stamping on every beat until the end.